Unconditional
"Straight from the Heart"

Unconditional
"Straight from the Heart"

Kuhrizma Clemons

iUniverse, Inc.
Bloomington

Unconditional
"Straight from the Heart"

iUniverse books may be ordered through booksellers or by contacting:

iUniverse
1663 Liberty Drive
Bloomington, IN 47403
www.iuniverse.com
1-800-Authors (1-800-288-4677)

ISBN: 978-1-4759-8535-1 (sc)
ISBN: 978-1-4759-8536-8 (ebk)

Printed in the United States of America

iUniverse rev. date: 04/15/2013

Contents

LOVE OR HATE . . . . IT'S A THIN LINE

A FEW SNIPPETS

TIME TO MEET THE AUTHOR

Acknowledgments

I'd like to give a grateful thanks and acknowledgment to my mom and dad for their extraordinary support. To my BFF, Mariah, who helped me along the way and encouraged me to believe in myself. Also a huge shout out to all my English teachers @ Oceanway Middle School who told me to never give up and to never say never. All in all, these wonderful people helped me strive to meet my full potential. ☺

Nature
and
It's Beauty

Big Old Lazy Tree

Big Old Lazy Tree,
Won't you come dance with me?
Swishing, swaying in the wind,
Won't you awake and be my friend?
We will jump up to the sky,
Hear the big blue ocean cry.
Sing by night, dance by day,
Why won't you wake up to play?
We will jump, we'll dance, we'll twirl,
We will hop, we'll prance, and we'll whirl.
It's just you, It's just me,
Wake up Big Old Lazy Tree.

Butterfly

Love is like a butterfly.

It floats above thick, grassy fields.

You chase after it, trying to catch it but it continuously slips

from your grasp.

You finally stop chasing and let it come to you.

Suddenly, it lands upon the tip of your finger.

You cannot capture it, but only admire its beauty.

It then flies away.

It is now out of your sight.

You can no longer see it but you can still feel that tingling

sensation left upon your fingertip, like forbidden love leaving a

stinging sensation upon your fluttering heart.

Catch the Moonlight

If I could catch the moonlight,
It's the first thing that I'd do.
I would also catch the sunshine,
And then give it all to you.
Me and you,
You and I,
We will jump up to the sky.
Watching the stars twirl and dance,
I caught the moonlight,
Now it's in your hands.

Confused Flower of Beauty

When you're staring blankly through the vague vision of those cherry-colored glasses, everything seems beautiful to you. But I am not who you think I am. I'm not the sky that holds the world together, keeps it in one piece. But instead, I'm the lonely little grey cloud that sits hopelessly in the sky's arms, looking towards the moon for support, for assurance. Nor am I the fire that holds tightly on to the wood, rising up high with confidence, gallantly dancing across the calm night sky. But instead I am the wood, surrounded by the blazing fire, being protected from the cool, cold world with its warmth, hoping that the flames will never smother. You would be able to see who I really am if you would depart from the world of confusion. It's as if you're strolling down a silent cave with a flashlight but instead of using it, you continue walking through the cave in complete darkness. Oh how I wish you could see me for who I really am.

Nature's Fury

The oceans dance throughout the night,
My aching heart wraps your love tight.
The crazy leaves fight with the wind,
The light brown sand hollers and spins.
The demanding sky just sits and stares,
And the happy sun doesn't even care.

Speck of Dust

●◆●

Sometimes it feels like I'm a little doll on a big shelf.
But no matter how difficult things may get,
I'll always know that all my close friends and family love me. I'll
keep them wrapped in my heart.
Even on the days I feel like a speck of dust aimlessly floating
through the air.
A speck of dust that can only be seen when a shaft of light hits
it.

The Sky's Sorrow

◆

The sky's tears hit the pavement repeatedly, in unison with
mine.
My heart skips a beat with every strike of lightning that burns
the sky.
Clouds like lost ghosts, floating around aimlessly.
The sun like dust, fading into the abyss of darkness,
Along with my soul, drowning in sorrow.

Colors
Of
Time

RED

Red is my best friends name.
Red are the eyes of a bear untamed.
Red is the color of my bedroom wall,
Red are the leaves on the ground in the fall.
Red is the hair on my best friends head,
My friends favorite color, you've guessed it, it's red.
Red is the face of a child that fails,
Red is not the face of a vampire, it's pale.
Red are the cheeks of a child that has froze,
Red is the sun painting the sky with rose.
Red is the color of the polish on my toes,
Red is the heart that beats within the soul.

BLUE

Blue are the waves of the ocean.

Blue is the sky.

Blue are the jays flying up high.

Blue are the raspberries growing on the trees.

Blue is how I feel strolling through Earth's breeze.

Blue is the feeling you get when you're sad.

Feeling blue is the opposite of glad.

Blue is not green.

When you're feeling blue, you don't wanna be seen.

The blues go around every single day.

When you're feeling blue, I don't know what to say.

When I'm feeling blue, all I do is cry.

I gaze at the comforting ocean and sky.

Me and you.

Always feeling sad and blue.

The Love of
Family & Friends

Best Friends

Best friends are the greatest.
You know they are when the only times they make you cry is
when you're laughing too hard.
A best friend is someone who lends a shoulder when you need
to cry or just when you're sad, someone to calm your nerves
whenever you're mad.
They're always there whenever you need help; they love you
when you forget to love yourself.
They're the only ones to take away misery and make you laugh,
Best friends are like four leaf clovers, hard to find but lucky to
have. They are always awesome and so incredible,
They make bad times good and good times unforgettable.
They make you feel special, make your heart flip,
Give commendation for the power of friendship. ☺

Make it Last

You gotta live, love, laugh throughout the years.
One simple smile can hide a thousand tears.
Let the rules remain broken, but all promises kept.
To reach distant places, just take the first step.
Enjoy this good life and just make it last.
Create your own future, let go of the past.
If you don't have knowledge, then how will you know, to let the
abyss of everything go?
Forget about the world and just go with the flow.

*This was written in dedication to my big Brother at his graduation
dinner 6/16/12. Congrats big brother*

Amor de Familia

(Love of Family)

I love my family very much
They help me through my ups and downs.
My dad is like the sun—he shines light down on you so you can
live long and survive in this world.
My mom is like the beautiful clouds—she throws raindrops
down upon your fruit when you need the nourishment.
My brothers are like the wind—they can help push and pull you
to where you need to go. They run air in and out of your lungs
and make sure your heart doesn't stop jumping up and down.
My sister is like the moon - she guides the little stars around in
the solid sky to help them know where to stand in the world.

Familia, amor y apreciarlas mientras puedas, sé que lo hago.
(Family, love them and cherish them while you can, I know I do)

Friends and Family

❦

I love my friends and family,
O baby yes I do.
I love my friends and family,
And maybe you should too.
I love it when they make me laugh,
Although at times they make me cry.
I love it when they tell the truth,
Although some times they lie.
We always spend our time together,
Through the sunshine and the stormy weather.
I never, ever take them for granted,
Love is where my heart is planted.
We may see face to face, but not always eye to eye,
Show a little love, it's not that hard to try.
They are elaborate.
Sometimes they love & sometimes they hate.
Will my heart contaminate?
It's not vague but it's very easy to see . . .
I love my friends and my family!

Love
or
Hate . . . .
It's A Thin Line

Leap into Motherhood

In my arms, it's you I hold.
You cry out loud with lungs so bold.
Oh, so bold, just like my love.
My sweet angel sent from above.
You're in my heart forever more. Aching with love down to the
core.
I need you as you need me.
Open those little eyes so you can see.
Grasp my finger with your hand,
And I just know you understand.
Taking this step into motherhood . . .
Doing what no other could.

-Dedicated to all mothers, especially the first-timers. ☺

Crystal Eyes

When you looked into my eyes, shining like diamonds,
The silent bleeding tears of my soul were finally seized.
But my heart had a mind of it's own.
It made a feeble attempt to drown itself in contentment,
Proving that those idle diamond eyes were nothing but shattered
crystals.
It seems I waited for you only to be thrown and trapped in
complete darkness and confusion.

Prisoner of Love

●◆●

I watch as you kick rocks,
I watch you kick the dust.
I gazed into your eyes,
But they were filled with lust.
My heart was filled with love,
My eyes like tiny doves.
I should've known that you'd betray me,
But my vision was so vague.
Your love was like Black Death,
It spread like the Bubonic Plague.
You knew that I was senseless,
But still you took control.
You took away my heart,
And you captured my poor soul.
But still I'll remember you,
From January to December.
Terrified to forget yet forbidden to remember.
I'll keep in mind from year to year,
To love without limits and dream without fear.

Candlelight Presence

● ◆ ●

You're the only reason our love burned like a candle's light in
the dark of the night.
You were the one to seal the deep hole in my heart.
You were there to seize the silent bleeding tears of my shallow
soul.
I loved the way you held me day and night in the safety of your
arms.
The moon crept up at the break of dawn, careful not to disrupt
the sky, holding us closely in its presence.

Runaway Love

Love without limits,
Dream without fear.
Armo as if you're
never gonna shed a tear.
Believe in yourself,
Listen to your heart.
It's about where we end,
Not 'bout where we start.
Live like you're dying,
Set yourself free.
Fly into the sky,
And sail into the sea.
Take hold of my hand,
And we'll run away.
We will not return,
Yet we aren't going to stay.
Just look at the sky that lives up above,
Take hold of my hand, we'll run away, my love.

Living in the Present

◆

Drowning in a sea of regrets.
Floating on top of memories that only seem to fade to dust.
Trying to fix what broke on it's own.
You cannot rewind the past, you cannot fast forward the future.
So let life just unfold by living in the present,
Just press play.

I Love You

I will love you 'til the sun doesn't pop up in the sky,
I will love you 'til the trees and the flowers all die.
I will love you 'til the grass turns pink, orange, and yellow,
I will love you 'til the waves in the ocean won't flow.
I will love you 'til the moon doesn't shine so bright,
I'll love you 'til the stars won't twinkle at night.
I will love you 'til the trees won't dance in the wind.
I will love you till the moon and the planets won't spin,
I will love you 'til the dazed in the world get a clue,
I will always and forever love you.

When Love Comes into Your Life

Every time I see you,

I fall in love all over again.

When you smile at me,

Electricity ricochets through my bones.

I want you to want me,

I need you to need me.

But most of all I want and need you to trust me when I say I

love you, cause I will always mean it.

Just think of how different it would be if you had never met the

one person who changed everything.

Unlovable Love

◆

When you're the one who made me fall,
Why won't you catch me?
You made me fall so in love,
That I could hardly breathe.
I wanna feel your kiss again,
Soar into the night.
I wanna hear your voice again,
I'm turning off the lights.
The lights of love is what I mean,
I'll just roam through life, unheard, unseen.
They say to listen to your heart,
I did that thing right from the start.
Our love was not a work of art.
I guess gravity isn't the only thing that keeps you down,
I'll wait for you to come back around.

Love Sick Despair at Midnight

Every night I dream of strolling on the warm and sandy beach.
Watching as the big waves of the dark blue ocean jump up and
gallantly dance across the star-filled sky. I don't know what
tomorrow holds, but I know who holds tomorrow. I'll be waiting
for you, thinking of you, together we belong.

The Crazy Thing we Call Love

What is love?

Is it just a word?

Or is it an emotion expressed by one's true feelings?

Something that holds people together, something so strong it
can mend broken hearts.

The thing that defines a true relationship.

The one thing that can make one feel dumb, restless, or insecure.

Everyone deserves love but not everyone gets it.

Love shouldn't be played as a game, nor taken for granted.

It should be respected with true ways of the heart.

Love is so powerful it can never fail.

Love cannot go unnoticed but it can go untamed.

Why do we love love when love seems to hate us?

Praise for crazy, stupid, love.

Broken Hearts & Shattered Love

•◆•

The ocean and sky cry in unison, throwing their rage upon the earth. My soul and I mourn together as you toss your anger upon me. I don't reject the words that are slung towards my heart, piercing it harshly, causing it to flutter to the ground and shatter to pieces. You stare carelessly at the mess you've made, a mess I can never clean up. I watch you stroll away, spilling your harmful terms all over the place, drowning in them with regret and me in sorrow. As I successfully collect my broken heart off the hungry, parched ground, I carefully place the pieces back together. And at that moment, something inside me yawns and stretches and slowly starts to come back to life. Completely out of nowhere, this tidal wave of contentment comes crashing down over me. I turn towards the suicidal palm fronds, stepping into the undiscerning world as the sun dusts the sky with rose.

Echo of my Soul

● ◆ ●

You don't even know what's through the window of my soul.
When you look into the mirror, the truth will slowly fade, but
the lies will get clearer.
The rosy glass is still fixed. Your image is broken,
You never even heard a single word I have spoken.
I am still trying to reach out for your hand,
The battlefield of love is where we used to stand.
I guess maybe my love was no good at all,
I thought our love was perfect but then we hit a wall.
Can't you hear the whispers crawling down your neck?
Can't you see that it is time for you to draw from the deck?
Your eyes and ears are fooling you,
You go through life without a clue.
Like a bull, my heart is bold. You left me standing in the cold,
Can't you hear the echoing of my shattered soul?

False Love

I thought you were my best friend, But you don't even know me.
You turned and stabbed me in the back and you confused my
dreams.
You went and betrayed my trust,
Our old memories fade to dust.
Your heart is very cold,
So cold that now I'm freezing.
You couldn't see into my soul, you had stopped believing.
I thought you were my lover. I thought you were my friend.
The trust is gone. The love is gone. Now we are at an end.
It's time, it's time to say goodbye,
Now you're free, go ahead and fly.
Just leave my heart like a clinched fist.
Your commitment is what I really miss.
Now we're finished, now we're through,
You hate me but yet, I still love you.

Waiting for Eternal Love

I sit here, staring up at the big blue sky, watching as the sun burst from behind the white fluffy clouds, revealing it's bright sunlight. Lying in the warm grass, wishing my beloved was here by my side, singing sweetly in my ear, as the cool wind blows through our hair. Oh, how I wish that magic rainbow could send me across to where you are . . . so we can be together for the rest of eternity.

Slowly Fading Love

I wish I didn't fall in love too easily. I wished my love
for you would slowly fade, but it hasn't.
I want you to love me like you love her.
I'm sorry but I'm not going to sit here and wait for you and
your love. It's kind of funny how someone can break your heart
and you still love them with all the little pieces. I guess mistakes
only make us stronger, which is why I'll never stop fighting for
you.

A few snippets

Stained

Silent words drip from your lips,
leaking all over the marble floors,
staining the tile and hurting my soul,
blotches of pain printed on my heart.

No one's youer than you

•━◆━•

Sometimes it's hard to follow your heart when everyone expects
something different from you.
People influence you; they try to change who you are.
But all in all, you have to believe and stay true to yourself.
Just be you. ☺

Young, Helpless Soul

◆

I design all my frowns to be disguised as smiles, all my pain disguised as happiness. But why should I pretend to be drenched in endless rays of sunshine, when in true reality, I'm soaked in gloomy shadows and 50 shades of grey?

There is indeed a secret treasure buried beneath my heart.

I yearn for you to dig it up and possess it with your love, to uncover this veil of mystery lingering over my brow, to lift this heavy weight off my shoulders. Is it so vague to see that my poor young soul needs someone's, anyone's compassion?

Time
to meet the author

Meet the Author

Kind, humble, and compassionate.
Lover of chocolate, long walks and warm summer nights.
Hardworking and determined,
Reserved but outgoing.
One devoted to truly being herself.
Just simply me. ☺

-Kuhrizma

Special Thanks

I would like to thank the following individuals:

~Mom & Dad for funding my life and my first and future book endeavors!

~Shannon Howard, for the amazing photos you always provide for my family and me.

~Tatiana Kitchen, for the amazing cover and portrait of me, your talent is extraordinary.

Printed in the United States
By Bookmasters